Everyman's Poetry

Everyman, I will go with thee,
and be thy guide

Heinrich Heine

Translated and edited by T. J. REED and DAVID CRAM

University of Oxford

EVERYMAN
J. M. Dent · London

J. M. Dent
Orion Publishing Group
Orion House
5 Upper St Martin's Lane,
London WC2H 9EA

Typeset by Deltatype Ltd, Birkenhead, Merseyside
Printed and Great Britain by
The Guernsey Press Co. Ltd., Guernsey, C. I.

British Library Cataloguing-in-Publication
Data is available upon request.

ISBN 0 460 87865 4

The translators and the publishers wish to thank Angel Books for permission
to use extracts from: Heinrich Heine, *Deutschland: A Winter's Tale*: Dual text
with translations, introduction and notes by T. J. Reed, Angel Books, London, 1997.

Contents

Note on the Author and Translators

HEINRICH HEINE's life (1797–1856), spent half in Germany and half in France, spans high Romanticism and the beginning realism of a Europe whose political shape and literary sensibility were transformed by war and successive revolutions. The poetry Heine writes is a fascinating mixture of beauty and irony, phantasy and reality, lyric and politics. The conflicts between these things are illuminated by the fireworks of his wit, which is a delight in itself but also a pointer to the issues of his time and beyond. What Heine has to say and the way he says it makes him a thoroughly modern European voice.

DAVID CRAM read Modern Languages at Brasenose College, Oxford, and subsequently migrated to the States for graduate study at Cornell University. On his return, he was for fourteen years head of the Department of Linguistics at Aberdeen University. Since 1988 he has been University Lecturer in Linguistics, and Fellow of Jesus College, Oxford.

JIM REED is Taylor Professor of German at Oxford University and a Fellow of the British Academy. His work includes books on Thomas Mann, Goethe and Schiller, and a translation of Heinrich Heine's long satirical poem *Germany: A Winter's Tale* (new bilingual edition 1997).

Chronology of Heine's Life

Year	Life
1797	Birth of Harry Heine (known as Heinrich after his baptism in 1825) on 13 December, to a Jewish family in Düsseldorf, the eldest of four children
1815	Apprentice in a banking firm in Frankfurt
1816	Employed in the banking firm of his uncle Salomon, in Hamburg

Chronology of his Times

Year	Cultural Context	Historical Context
1798	Wordsworth and Coleridge, *Lyrical Ballads*	Napoleon invades Egypt; Battle of the Nile
1804		Napoleon crowns himself emperor
1805	Death of Schiller	Battles of Trafalgar and Austerlitz
1806		England declares war on Prussia
		Napoleon occupies Berlin after the Battle of Jena, and abolishes the Holy Roman Empire, the loose confederation of German states founded in the Middle Ages
1807		Slave trade abolished in the British Empire
1808	Goethe, *Faust, Part I*	
1812		Napoleon's troops invade Russia; retreat from Moscow
1813–15		So-called 'Wars of Liberation', in which Germans joined in the fight against Napoleon
1815		Battle of Waterloo; defeat and overthrow of Napoleon
		Congress of Vienna
		Restoration of French monarchy
		Metternich, Austrian Chancellor, becomes the dominant figure in German politics

Year	Life
1818	The firm Harry Heine & Co. is established with the financial support of his uncle. It goes into liquidation the following year
1819–20	Study at the University of Bonn, where he is registered to read law. Schlegel sees Heine's early poems and encourages him
1820	Study at the University of Göttingen. He is rusticated for half a year on account of a duel
1821–23	Study at the University of Berlin. Attends philosophy lectures by Hegel. Extends his circle of literary acquaintances at the salon of Varnhagen von Ense and his wife Rahel Levin
1821	Publication by Maurer in Berlin of Heine's first collection of verse, *Poems* (*Gedichte*), which is well received
1822	Start of his collaboration with the Association for Judaic Culture. Visit to Poland
1823	Publication of *Tragedies with a Lyrical Intermezzo* (*Tragödien nebst einem lyrischen Intermezzo*)
1824	Resumes study at Göttingen. Walking tour through the Harz mountains
1825	Protestant baptism in Heiligenstadt. Doctoral degree from the University of Göttingen. Proposes marriage to his cousin Therese Heine in Hamburg, but this is not allowed by her father
1826	First contact with the firm of Hoffman and Campe (Hamburg) who publish all of Heine's subsequent works that appear in Germany. Publication of the first volume of *Travel Pictures* (*Reisebilder*)
1827	Summer visit to London and Ramsgate. Publication of *Book of Songs* (*Buch der Lieder*) and the second volume of *Travel Pictures*
1828	In Munich, where he attempts unsuccessfully to gain a chair in the history of literature at the University. Suffers from severe depression after hearing that Therese Heine, his earlier love, has married

Year	Cultural Context	Historical Context
1817	Keats, *Endymion* Mary Shelley, *Frankenstein*	
1819		Zollverein (Customs Union) instituted by Prussia Carlsbad decrees; repression of ideas in German universities
1822	Death of Shelley	Greek Declaration of Independence
1824	Death of Byron in Greece	
1825		Opening of Stockton to Darlington Railway
1827	Death of William Blake and of Beethoven	

Year	Life
1829	In Berlin, where he makes the acquaintance of Achim von Armin, Bettina Brentano and Felix Mendelssohn-Bartholdy. Publication of the third volume of *Travel Pictures*
1830	Trip to Heligoland, where he first hears news of the July Revolution in France
1831	Move to Paris, which becomes his permanent residence for the remainder of his life and where he makes acquaintance with Balzac, Berlioz, Chopin, Dumas, Hugo, Liszt, Nerval, George Sand and others
1832	Publication of *Conditions in France* (*Französische Zustände*)
1834	First acquaintance with Eugénie Mirat ('Mathilde'), a sales girl in a Paris shoe shop, whom he marries in 1841
1835	Heine's writings are banned in Germany
1836	Publication of *The Romantic School* (*Die Romantische Schule*)
1841	Marriage to Mathilde. Heine wounded in a duel
1843	Trip to Hamburg. First acquaintance with Karl Marx later in the year in Paris
1844	Second trip to Hamburg (July-October). Death of Heine's uncle Salomon (December), whose will, contrary to Heine's expectations, fails to provide him with a pension. Friedrich Engels publishes a

Year	Cultural Context	Historical Context
1829		British Catholic Emancipation Act
1830		Second French Revolution; abdication of Charles X
1831	Death of Hegel	
1832	Death of Goethe and of Sir Walter Scott	Reform Bill passed in England
1837		Queen Victoria succeeds to the throne
1838	First edition of Martin Tupper's *Proverbial Philosophy*	*Great Western* steamer crosses Atlantic
1839		Invention of photographic camera by Louis Daguerre
1840		Marriage of Queen Victoria to her cousin Prince Albert of Saxe-Coburg
		Penny postage instituted
1843	Wordsworth succeeds Southey as Poet Laureate	

Year	Life
	translation of Heine's poem *The Weavers* in the journal *New Moral World*, as part of an article headed 'Rapid Progress of Communism in Germany', adding 'Henry Heine, the most eminent of all living German poets, has joined our ranks'
1844	Publication of *New Poems (Neue Gedichte)*, together with *Germany: A Winter's Tale (Deutschland, Ein Wintermärchen)*
1845	First stroke, with partial paralysis
1847	Publication of *Atta Troll, A Summer Night's Dream (Atta Troll, Ein Sommernachtstraum)*
1848	Heine collapses in the Louvre (according to legend, in front of the Venus de Milo). He becomes permanently confined to bed, his 'mattress grave'
1849–50	Heine's sight grows worse. His secretary, Karl Hillebrand, takes down the poems of the *Romanzero* from dictation, and reads to him from Goethe's works and from the Bible
1851	Publication of the collection *Romanzero*. Campe sells 30,000 copies within four months
1854	Publication of *Miscellaneous Writings (Vermischte Schriften)* in three volumes, which includes the section *Poems, 1853 and 1854 (Gedichte, 1853 und 1854)*. Publication in London of *Selections from the Poetry of Heinrich Heine*, translated by John Stores Smith ('John Ackerlos')
1855	Thirteenth edition of the *Book of Songs*

Year	Cultural Context	Historical Context
1845	Death of the critic August Wilhelm Schlegel First performance of Wagner's *Tannhäuser*	
1846		Repeal of British Corn Laws
1848	Marx, *Communist Manifesto* John Stuart Mill, *The Principles of Political Economy*	The Year of Revolutions: insurrections in France, Ireland, Italy, Spain, Germany, Hungary and Austria
1849	Death of Chopin in Paris	
1850	Death of Wordsworth and Balzac	Submarine telegraph cable laid between England and France
1851	Death of the artist Turner	Great Exhibition in London
1852		Louis Napoleon proclaimed Emperor, Napoleon III
1854		Start of Crimean War

Year	Life
1856	Death of Heine on 17 February; burial in the cemetery of Montmartre on 20 February, attended by Théophile Gautier, Alexandre Dumas, Alexander Weill, among others. Publication in London of *Heinrich Heine's Book of Songs*, translated by J. E. Wallis
1859	Publication in London of *The Poems of Heine, Complete*, with translations by E. A. Bowring
1869	Posthumous publication of *Last Poems and Meditations* (*Letzte Gedichte und Gedanken*)

Year	Cultural Context	Historical Context
1859	Darwin, *Origin of Species* Marx, *Das Kapital*	

Introduction

Heine is one of Germany's great poets, but in no straightforward way. His diction and form are simple and traditional, but he has a complex and divided mind, and the fascination of his writing lies in the way traditional simplicity manages to render modern complexity and division. The effect can be moving, and it can also – not a usual feature of lyrical poetry – be very funny. The two effects are often simultaneous, which is more intriguing still. Heine's ironic wit would stand out even in a less generally earnest context than German culture. But the irony is not gratuitous and free-floating. It has roots in the disharmonies and conflicts of his day, and it drew his poetry in the end irresistibly (though he resisted for a long time) into politics. All of which has often been, and sometimes still is, deeply disapproved of in Germany. He is no uncontroversial classic.

Heinrich Heine was born in 1797 to Jewish parents in the Rhineland city of Düsseldorf. The timing meant he grew up in two discordant worlds at once, the world of the Romantic literary imagination and that of post-revolutionary Europe. His poetic sensibility was formed by the Romantic taste for folksong simplicity, fairy-tale fantasy, and a mistily perceived Germanic medieval past. At the same time his sense of reality was formed by the changes, and the efforts to reverse them, that shaped and reshaped Europe in the years between 1789 and 1815: first the French Revolution and the Napoleonic Wars, then the Restoration of the old European order and the suppression of liberal ideas after Napoleon's final defeat at Waterloo. This political world was as uncompromisingly hard as the poetic world was seductively soft. The two offered a choice of Real and Unreal between which no compromise was possible; they were the horns of a dilemma that was to last half Heine's creative life: should poetry confront reality or evade it?

Heine began by learning the Romantic poetic game, learning both to love and to use it. His first collection, *Book of Songs* (*Buch der Lieder*) of 1827, revels in the manipulation of Romantic rhymes, rhythms, images and stock themes – love, nature, dream, a never-

never past. Whatever else Heine was or later became, he was first of all a consummate Romantic poet. Many of his early poems are wholly untouched by irony, reenactments of Romantic sensibility so perfect that they go beyond mere imitation or pastiche (e.g. 'Death is the Night . . .'). Poems like these inspired superb settings by the great Lieder composers: Schumann's cycle *Dichterliebe* (*A Poet in Love*) and his Opus 24 Song Sequence, or the handful of pieces that make up Schubert's *Schwanengesang* (*Swansong*) – he only discovered Heine's poetry a short while before dying – and include one of his most dramatic settings, 'The Double'.

But Heine also learned to mistrust Romanticism and all its works, above all for what it left unsaid about modern life, though the lesson was forced upon him more by what it said – and what he too often found himself saying – about those stock themes, in those set forms. Later he would look back on this learning process and his revolt against what he had learned and turn it into a typical piece of word-play, speaking of 'the Romantic School, where I spent the most agreeable years of my youth and ended up by beating the schoolmaster' (Foreword to *Atta Troll*). This was not quite the violent revolt the words suggest, more a creeping subversion clearest in the tone, which is that of a sceptical, hard-bitten modern equally to be heard in Byron, whom Heine once called 'my cousin'. From early in *Book of Songs*, there are poems that undo the convention they inhabit. An ironic intelligence ends dreams in harsh awakenings, it peers out from behind the 'natural' scenery, and doubts the idyll of love. Heine was probably helped here by the rigours of a real love-affair: the portrait of the lady in his lover's complaint feels too distinctive to be fiction – on that we can probably take the poem 'Figments' at its word. There was also no getting away from the un-Romantic realities of being a poor relation with more debts than prospects (see 'Principles'). Yet for all the ironic breaking of mood in these poems, they do not merely debunk a superseded literary fashion. Repeated satire on *passé* poetry would have palled on the writer before it ever filled a volume and reached the reader. The paradox of the early Heine is that his doubts about Romanticism never wholly undid its original imprinting effect. For better or worse, Romanticism was part of him. So when he sketches a typical scene – say, an impassioned young man on his knees before his beloved, or a nature-lover among hills and woods and water – only to pull the carpet from under them and question how trustworthy the lady's love or nature's beauty is, it is not just cold cerebral destruction. Rather he is yoking the discordant halves of his sensibility together in a single bitter-sweet but honest utterance. Sometimes a kind of double-bluff turns irony against irony and virtually cancels it out: the poet discovers that the Romantic play-acting he has seen through was after all a mask for true feeling (see 'High Time'). What other, more real face was there to wear?

If irony could not finally demolish Romantic convention, nor could it construct a new poetic mode to replace it, and if Heine was ever to get out of his dilemma, he needed new themes or new forms, preferably both. At the end of *Buch der Lieder*, he experiments with free-verse seascapes inspired by a stay on the North Sea island of Norderney. But this, poetically too, was no more than a holiday. There were limits to how often you could describe the sea before it became another cliché. Something new did offer, but not in poetry. Even before *Book of Songs* appeared, Heine had published the first of his *Travel Sketches*, wonderfully light and humorous descriptive-cum-reflective reworkings of a pattern Laurence Sterne set in his *Sentimental Journey*. Over the next few years this mode really did give Heine a new freedom, both in theme – he could digress from the line of travel to talk about anything he liked, including politics, which a dozy censor might not even notice; and also in form: 'prose', he rejoiced, 'has taken me into its broad embrace'. What is more, when in 1831 he went into voluntary exile in Paris, partly for political reasons, he found a ready-made vocation for his brilliant prose pen in explaining French politics to the Germans and German culture to the French.

But at root he was a poet, so what about poetry? Heine had a taboo over using it for political purposes, however much politics occupied his mind and filled his prose. Poetry, in his still ultimately Romantic conception, was a higher realm and must remain that. So poetically he marked time, still going through the motions of *Book of Songs* in a cycle he rather sanguinely called *New Spring*. France did briefly give him a new angle on love – new for Heine that is, though conventional enough in itself. If Romanticism had to mean unrequited passion, Paris in an equally clichéd way had to mean sensual adventure. A cycle headed *Miscellaneous* (miscellaneous women, not poems) celebrated his release from non-fulfilment in a sequence of casual affairs, real or imagined (see 'Thanksgiving', 'New faith'). But sensuality, like the sea, had its poetic limits, at least for Heine, and this awareness, like his earlier ironies, infiltrated sensual celebration itself. Before the Mardi Gras high of passion is well over, the poet is already brooding on tomorrow's penitence ('Ash Wednesday').

It is ironic that, after all his youthful yearnings, sensual pleasure leaves the poet unfulfilled, even bored. He seems positively to need the ashes of existential bitterness, like the hero of his knightly legend 'Tannhäuser'. That strange poem begins as a tale of sin and damnation in the style of early folk-ballad (Heine knew the authentic version in a famous folksong collection of the day) but tails off into racy satirical travelogue. It can be read as an allegory of Heine's own situation in Paris. 'I am Tannhäuser in the Venusberg', he told a visitor ruefully. If we set beside that the poem 'Noncombatant', chosen as prologue to the 1843 *New Poems* (*Neue Gedichte*) which contain his whole poetic output since 1827, then it seems clear that the 'bitterness' Tannhäuser/Heine needed was the engagement of his poetry with the political realities of the day.

Such an engagement still does not come about before there has been a final fling of Heine's dyed-in-the-wool Romantic self. Bizarrely, the first of his two long satirical poems, *Atta Troll*, is directed not at any political target but at the way political targets were being missed – so Heine thought – by other writers, even though these were people whose politics Heine shared (as far, that is, as he ever agreed with anyone). He mocks their clumsy efforts in the figure of a subversive escaped dancing bear. Not surprisingly, they accused him of political unreliability: he had 'talent' but not 'character'. Yet *Atta Troll* was also, as he said, the 'last free woodland song of Romanticism'; it marks the end of an inhibition and the start of a more practical response to other people's bad political poetry: show them how it *should* be done! The Midsummer Night's Dream of an allegorical bear is followed by the Winter's Tale of a real return to Germany after more than a decade of exile. Like the last section of 'Tannhäuser' which tailed away in a promise to tell us more some other time, *Germany. A Winter's Tale* is (in Heine's phrase) 'versified travel-sketches', and it keeps Tannhäuser's promise. At last Heine is combining on a large scale the free-ranging movement of his prose with the poetic tricks of his old Romantic trade. There are dreams and visions, ghosts and doubles, a medieval cathedral and a medieval emperor, but they are all now related to modern society and given a clear political point. Above all, the traditional Romantic verse-form has lost its innocence and come into its own in a new way. Compared with the *Hiawatha*-like verse of *Atta Troll*, audibly non-committal with its floating trochee rhythms and no rhymes, the simple folksong stanza proves the perfect form for satire. Its iambic rhythm only needs a few dactyls thrown in to get the relaxed conversational tone of the travelling man-of-the-world, and at stanza's end there is rhyme – often outrageous rhyme in the manner of Byron's *Don Juan* – to make the point and to give a victim the *coup de grâce*.

And besides the sustained performance of *Germany. A Winter's Tale*, Heine rounds off *New Poems* with a cycle called *Zeitgedichte* – 'poems for the times'. In them he taunts his own side – the inert German populace ('No Need to Worry', 'Promise') and the cautiously vague liberals ('The Political Poets'), he makes scurrilous attacks on royal personages ('King Ludwig to King Frederick William IV'), and he writes in grim earnest about the most brutal acts of oppression committed against starving workers ('The Silesian Weavers').

But the 1848 revolutions across continental Europe – in France, Germany, Austro-Hungary – all failed. 'In October 1849' catches the mood of that moment. It is also the moment when Heine was struck down by illness. He spent eight years dying, confined to what he called his 'mattress grave'. Public and private experience drove him in on himself. There was bitterness now and to spare. Dreams and memories and visions of beauty and happiness mocked him. He cast a final cold eye on life, seeing his own defeat replicated in all the defeats of history and legend. He wrote lyrics of lament, pain and despair. They remained ironic, defiant, sometimes humorous.

T. J. REED

Note on the Texts and the Translations

There are no problems of variants and editions that need come between readers of this volume and the enjoyment of Heine. We print the poems in chronological order, as a continuous record of the poet in his time. In transferring him to ours, we have aimed at versions that will capture Heine's tone and temperament, if necessary by using modern equivalents. That is itself in Heine's own spirit – he was nothing if not a moderniser of poetry.

We indicate who is responsible for each translation by a single letter at the foot: D=David Cram; J=Jim Reed; and (in one case) A=Ann Reed. Most of the titles are ours. Heine's title or (where there is none) his first line is given alongside the English in the Contents, so that anyone who has the German and the curiosity can check our efforts against the original.

Heinrich Heine

Prologue

I walked into the fairy wood,
Where the moonlight casts a spell,
And the linden trees forever spread
Their sweet enchanted smell.

I wandered on, and as I walked   5
I heard from up above
The timeless nightingale which sits
And sings of sad-sweet love.

It sits and sings of sad-sweet love,
Of laughter mixed with tears,   10
Reviving long-forgotten dreams
From sad-sweet former years. –

I wandered on, and as I walked
Trees parted in the wood,
And there, with towering gabled walls,   15
A stately palace stood.

The windows were all shuttered up;
There was an eerie air
Of mournfulness and misery
As if death resided there.   20

A statue crouched before the door,
A hybrid of lust and dread,
With the claws and torso of a lion
And a woman's breasts and head.

The Sphinx's features bore the look   25
Of voluptuous sexual fire;
Her silent lips were round and full
And smiled with enthralling desire.

With the prompting of the nightingale
I was helpless to resist;   30
I kissed those lips that reached for me
Demanding to be kissed.

Slowly the statue came to life,
And the marble began to groan;
She sucked my kisses into her   35
With a thirst that made me moan.

She almost drank my breath away,
And then, aroused afresh,
She clasped me close, and with her claws
Began to tear my flesh.   40

The blissful torture grew intense
As pleasure vied with pain,
For while her kisses drove me wild
Her claws dug in again.

Meanwhile, the nightingale sang on: 45
O Sphinx! Why should it be
That you should mix such torment with
Your every ecstasy?

O Sphinx! I've pondered long and deep
As the centuries have evolved,   50
And yet however much I muse,
Your riddle stays unsolved.

                              D.

Belshazzar

Towards midnight now the hours moved on,
In silent sleep lay Babylon.

Only up in the castle there
The vassals shout, the torches flare.

Up in the hall of the mighty king, 5
Belshazzar's feast was in full swing.

His armoured men sat glittering round,
Goblet on goblet of wine they downed.

The goblets' clinking, the liegemen's cheer,
Are what the dour king likes to hear. 10

His face is flushed, his cheeks aglow,
The wine it makes his courage grow.

Blindly he's drawn beyond all bounds,
Till a sinful challenge to God resounds.

He boasts and blasphemes against the Lord, 15
To the roaring cheers of his servile horde.

The King commands with an eye that burns,
A servant hastens and returns.

With golden vessels his back is piled;
Jehovah's temple has been defiled. 20

And the King he seizes with hand of sin
A sacred vessel filled to the brim.

And he drains it hastily, drains it dry,
And with foaming mouth they hear him cry:

'Jehovah, your power is past and gone –   25
I am the King of Babylon.'

But scarce the awful word was said,
The King was stricken with secret dread.

The raucous laughter silent falls,
It is suddenly still in the echoing halls.   30

And see! as if on the wall's white space
A human hand began to trace,

Writing and writing across the stone
Letters of fire, wrote, and was gone.

The King sat still, with staring gaze,   35
His knees were water, ashen his face.

Fear chilled the vassals to the bone,
Fixed they sat and gave no tone.

Wise men came, but none was equipped
To read the sense of the fiery script.   40

Before the sun could rise again,
Belshazzar by his men was slain.

                                    J.

Spring Song (1)

In all the loveliness of May,
When every bud was swelling,
Oh then it was within me
The force of love came welling.

In all the loveliness of May,   5
When song birds were returning
Oh then it was I told her
My longing and my yearning.

                                                  A.

Death is the Night

Death is the night, the cool, cool night,
Life is the sultry day.
The dark comes on, I am weary;
Sleep draws me away.

Over my bed a tall, tall tree   5
And a nightingale. It seems
She is singing of love, of love, of love.
I hear it through my dreams.

                                                  J.

Stood Up

Every morning fresh I wonder,
Will she come today?
Evening finds me still lamenting,
No, she stayed away.

Sleepless with my sorrow, somehow　　　　　　5
I get through the night;
Dreaming, half asleep, I wander
In the morning's light.

J.

Sorority

On a bright summer day in the garden,
　As I go for my morning walk,
The flowers are whispering softly,
　But I'm in no mood to talk.

The flowers are whispering softly,　　　　　　5
　As softly as ever they can:
'Pray God he's not hard on our sister,
　That gaunt-eyed, grim young man.'

D.

Love's Declensions

For aeon after aeon
Up in the skies above
The stars gaze at each other
With unrequited love.

The language they converse in   5
Is exquisitely grand,
And one no linguistician
Could ever understand.

I alone have learnt it,
Of all the human race,   10
By using as a textbook
The grammar of your face.

D.

Dream Meeting

Each night I see you wave to me
When in my dreams we meet;
I moan aloud and throw myself
Before your pretty feet.

You look at me and shake your head　　　　5
And breathe a soulful sigh;
A teardrop like a priceless pearl
Trickles from your eye.

You say a secret whispered word
And hand me a cypress spray.　　　　10
But when I wake, the spray is gone,
And the word just fades away.

D.

Figments

Dearest, tell me, aren't you really
Just some image from a dream
Of the kind with which on sultry
Days a poet's brain-cells teem?

Ah, but such sweet lips as yours are,   5
Looks of love with witchcraft blent,
Such a darling, such a vision –
That no poet could invent.

Vampires, basilisks and dragons,
Monsters in their hideous den,   10
Yes, such beasts of fable can be
Conjured by the poet's pen.

But you, dearest, and your malice
And your face all innocent
And your sweet and treacherous glances –   15
That no poet could invent.

                                        J.

Desperately Seeking . . .

God knows where the crazy woman's
Found herself a place to stay;
I've been looking for her in this
Cursèd rain for half the day.

Trying this hotel and that one,   5
Running till I'm out of puff,
Asking waiters if they've seen her,
All I get is 'No, sir', 'Tough'.

There! she's waving from that window,
Giggling in her girlish voice.   10
Sweetie, how could I know you'd be
Staying somewhere quite so choice?

J.

Sweet-bitter

The linden blossomed, the nightingale sang,
The sun was shining its genial best.
You kissed me, and your arm went round me,
Pressing me close to your swelling breast.

The leaves came down, the raven croaked,   5
The sun was gone from a gloomy sky.
You curtsied the coldest curtsey you could.
We frostily bade each other goodbye.

J.

Gloomy-Go-Round

John's in love with Mary,
But Mary falls for Fred;
He too is quite contrary
And plumps for Jane instead.

Mary, piqued, will marry   5
Any Tom or Dick
Or (as it happens) Harry.
John feels jolly sick.

The old tale doesn't vary
Although the names are new;   10
And if *you're* John or Mary
It breaks your heart in two.

D.

Hide-and-Seek

We've been close as twins for all of our lives,
As close as a proper sister and brother.
As children we often played 'husbands-and-wives'
But we never battered or hurt each other.
Later on, in our teens, we'd remember this,   5
And we'd tease one another with a hug or a kiss.
Or else, going out for a country walk,
We'd play 'hide-and-seek' as well as talk.
In the end, we were playing the game so well
That where we were hiding, we never could tell.   10

D.

Blessing

You look so like a flower,
So pure and undefiled,
It grips me with fear and sadness
Deep down inside, my child.

I feel I should speak a blessing   5
And touch your head, my child:
God help this lovely creature
To stay so undefiled.

                                        D.

The Fir Tree

On a barren arctic mountain,
The ice and snow lie deep,
And an isolated fir tree
Is nodding off to sleep.

It's dreaming of a palm tree,   5
In some exotic land,
That's pining away on a mountain
Of barren desert sand.

                                        D.

Reflections (1)

Hills and castles are reflected
In the mirror of the Rhine.
Gaily sails my little vessel,
All around the sunbeams shine.

Calm I watch the golden waters   5
Play and ripple at our keel.
And I feel within me stirring
All the things I used to feel.

Stream that lures with friendly welcome,
Promising profound delight,   10
I know better – surface glitter
Hides beneath it death and night.

Lovely show, but full of malice –
That is just my loved one's style!
She, like you, seems oh so friendly,   15
With her butter-wouldn't smile.

                              J.

The Lorelei

What is it that fills me with sadness,
And weighs down my spirits like lead?
An old story that drives me to madness
For I can't get it out of my head.

Through the gorge, a deep river is flowing;　　　　5
The air cools, soon day will be done;
Westwards, the cliff-tops are glowing
In the rays of the setting sun.

And then, if you lift your eyes higher,
You can pick out a figure up there:　　　　10
Her jewels are shining like fire,
And she's combing her long golden hair.

Her combing is slow and erotic,
And so is the flow of her song;
The melody's strangely hypnotic,　　　　15
And her voice is compellingly strong.

The man at the helm gives a shiver
As fear strikes his heart like a stone.
He's now blind to the rocks in the river;
She transfixes his eyes with her own.　　　　20

That then is the story's sad ending,
And the helmsman's as well, I'd surmise;
And if anyone's case needs defending
It is the Lorelei's.

D.

By the Fisherman's Cottage

We sat by the fisherman's cottage,
Gazing towards the sea;
The evening mists on the foreshore
Were gathering patchily.

From the lighthouse, as it darkened,   5
There came a beam of light,
And away on the far horizon
A ship hove into sight.

We talked about storms and shipwrecks
And the sailor's way of life,   10
Slung between sea and heaven,
And blended of pleasure and strife.

We talked about distant countries
From Thailand to Peru;
And of strange, exotic peoples,   15
And the curious things they do.

On the Ganges the air is scented
By the blossoms of giant trees;
And in front of lotus flowers
They worship on bended knees.   20

In Lapland the people are grubby,
Broad-mouthed and flat-headed and small;
They crouch round the fire baking fishes,
And shout at each other and brawl.

The girls had been listening intently,   25
Now silence descended at last.
In the meantime the ship had vanished;
Darkness was gathering fast.

D.

Noblesse Oblique

The seasons come and the seasons go,
    The generations too;
And even you may never know,
    My love, that I love you.

Perhaps before my dying day   5
    I'll get down on one knee
And simply have the guts to say
    'Please will you . . . come to tea?'

D.

Table Talk

They conversed as they sipped their Darjeeling,
(About love, as a matter of fact,)
The ladies with some depth of feeling,
And the gents with their usual tact.

'Affairs should be strictly platonic,'   5
The withered town councillor said;
And the smile from his wife was ironic,
As she wistfully nodded her head.

'Too much of the old rough-and-tumble
Is a health risk,' the major maintained.   10
The young lady was prompted to mumble
'How exactly . . . ?' But no one explained.

The deaconess spoke out forthrightly
On the topic of ecstasy;
And offered the bishop politely   15
Some more of the *excellent* tea.

There was one empty place at the table,
And one person, my poppet, too few.
There should have been someone there able
To hold forth on the subject like you.   20

D.

The Same Old Story

It's stormy, and it's pouring
A mixture of snow and sleet;
I sit by the window, brooding,
And watching the darkened street.

And then, from around the corner,   5
I can pick out a small dim glow;
An old woman with a lantern
Is crossing the street below.

She'll be buying a packet of flour
And some eggs and a pat of butter;   10
She's going to be baking a cake
For her grown-up little daughter,

Who's sitting at home by the fire,
Half-asleep in her comfy chair,
Her pretty face framed by the wavelets   15
Of her flowing golden hair.

D.

Another Drama

Hasn't she given the smallest hint
That shows she knows you're on the rack?
Can't you look into her eyes
To find out if she loves you back?

Can't you look into her eyes   5
And simply see into her soul?
In such affairs, my dear old chap,
The fool is not your usual role.

D.

They Loved One Another

They loved one another, but neither one
Was willing to confide.
They would both of them cut the other dead,
While dying of love inside.

Since they finally parted, now and then   5
They met up in their dreams, these two.
They had both of them long since wilted away,
And somehow they scarcely knew.

D.

The Double

The night is still, the streets are silent,
Here in this house my love once lived.
It's long since, now, that she left the city,
But the house still stands as it always did.

Someone is there, staring up at the windows,   5
Wringing his hands in the depths of his pain.
He turns this way, and horror grips me –
The moonlight shows me myself again!

You dreadful double, you pallid creature,
Why do you ape a lover's plight   10
Here on the spot where I went through torments
Long ago so many a night?

J.

The Three Wise Men

The Wise Men, coming from the East,
Kept asking every day:
'It's Bethlehem we're looking for;
Can someone show us the way?'

But no one ever seemed to know,   5
And the Wise Men plodded on,
Led only by the cheerful light
With which the lodestar shone.

And then at Joseph's house they heard
A quite almighty din;   10
The cattle mooed, the baby howled,
The Three Wise Men joined in.

                              D.

Reflections (2)

A vivid picture from the past
Flashes on my inner eye,
As if the moon were breaking through
The curtains of a cloudy sky.

Boating proudly down the Rhine   5
I was up on deck with everyone;
On either side the lush green banks
Were glowing in the evening sun.

A lovely face glowed golden too,
And just to make my joy complete,   10
I'd found a place where I could sit
Precisely at this lady's feet.

A lute was playing, songs were sung,
And the festive mood intensified;
The sky took on a deeper blue,   15
My spirits blossomed deep inside.

It was almost like a fairy tale
As castles, moors and woods slipped by,
And all of these shone crystal clear,
Reflected in the woman's eye.   20

D.

The Lay of the Modern Minstrel

What is the point, my dear buffoon,
Of harping on the same old tune?
Since laying love-eggs yet again
You've brooded like a bloody hen.

Each time you lay another batch   5
You cluck until the blighters hatch,
Only to disappear indoors
And clap them in that *book* of yours.

                              D.

You're in Love

You're in love, my dear old chap,
You can't laugh off the pain much longer;
It's getting murkier in your head
As in your heart the flame burns stronger.

You *are* in love, my dear old chap,   5
Although your ego wants to block it;
I see your heart's just burnt a hole
Right through your top left jacket pocket.

D.

The Castrati

The castrati all started tut-tutting
As soon as I'd sung the first bar;
They complained (and were really quite cutting!)
That my tone was too ballsy by far.

They themselves then began serenading,   5
And their timbre was tinglingly clear;
All around us their trills came cascading
Like a cut-glass chandelier.

They sang about love unrequited
(With full moon, I might add, and in June);   10
The ladies were simply delighted
As they sank in an exquisite swoon.

                                                    D.

A Double Life

Next door to me lives Don Henriquez,
Dubbed 'The Blade' by one and all;
In fact between my room and his
There's just a thin dividing wall.

The Salamancan ladies swoon   5
To see him striding down the street,
Equipped with spurs, a black moustache,
And gun dogs trotting at his feet.

It's strange, with such a ladies' man,
How ladyless his evenings are;   10
He sits at home alone and dreams
And on his knee sits his guitar.

And when he starts to pluck the strings
To yet another soulful air –
Dear *me*! the fretful songs he sings   15
Are just too close to home to bear.

D.

Brahms and Liszt, with Feeling

Love's blossoming here inside me
As we stroll beneath blossoming trees;
I've the feeling I'm walking on clouds, dear,
With rather wobbly knees.

I'm just worried I'm going to stumble   5
And go lurching against your breasts;
I'm legless with love, my darling,
And the garden's full of guests.

D.

Throwing Them off the Scent

You really needn't be afraid
My poems will give the game away.
Metaphors mean what *they* want
And never simply what they say.

Our secret love is buried deep   5
Beneath a barrow-load of roses.
In fact it's artfully concealed
Right underneath the public's noses.

And if the roses start to glow
Suspiciously – that's okey-doke!   10
These people don't believe in fire.
They'll think it's poetry. Just smoke.

D.

To Tell the Truth

When springtime comes, the sun and showers
Bring out a host of dancing flowers;
And when at night the moon peeps through,
The stars begin to twinkle too;
And when the bard sees two blue eyes,   5
Soulful songs materialise; –
But songs and stars and dancing flowers
And azure eyes and April showers,
However popular such stuff,
It's never *really* quite enough.   10

D.

High Time

It really is time I had the sense
To give up this endless moronic
Play-acting. I just can't go on
Being so histrionic.

The glorious backcloth was always daubed   5
In the high-Romantic fashion,
My knightly mantle shone like gold,
I felt the most exquisite passion.

Yet now that my melodramatic streak
Has been seen through with suitable cunning,   10
I feel as miserable as before,
As if the old play were still running.

O God! unknowing and in jest
I spoke my genuine feeling.
There was death in my breast when I merely thought   15
I was making a death-scene appealing.

                                        J.

Change of Tune

You yawned, and never said a thing,
On hearing how I was suffering;
Now hearing the same in soulful lyrics,
My word! you've changed to panegyrics.

D.

Condition

And once you are my lawful spouse,
You'll be envied beyond measure.
You'll do what you like the livelong day
And wallow in joys and pleasure.

Your scolding and raging will be for me.   5
No more than a matter of course.
But if you fail to praise my verse,
That will be grounds for divorce.

J.

World-view

When life and the world are all in pieces,
The German professor will have a thesis.
He can make sense of things when it matters,
Serve up a system for better or worse;
With his cast-off nightcaps and dressing-gown tatters   5
He'll stop up the holes in the universe.

J.

Principles

Better never mock the Devil,
Human life is very short,
And your precious soul's damnation
Isn't just an idle thought.

Better always pay your debtors,   5
Human life goes on and on,
And you'll have to borrow often,
Like you've borrowed all along.

J.

Philistines and Sophisticates

Philistines and bureaucrats,
And other narrow-minded prats
Are not amused at being mocked.
But wiser folk, we happy few,
Are happiest when the joke's on *you*.   5
(It doesn't do to show you're shocked.)

D.

True Love

I love you, dear old Rover,
And this you understand,
When I feed you titbits,
You'll come and lick my hand.

You're a doggedly honest creature,   5
And true to what you are;
My other friends (those humans)
All *try* too hard by far.

D.

Dusk, Sea

On the pallid sea-shore I sat,
Troubled by thoughts and alone.
The sun sank ever deeper, and cast
Glow-red stripes on the water,
And the white, wide waves   5
In the thrust of the tide
Foamed and roared nearer and nearer –
The strangest of sounds, a whisp'ring and piping,
Laughing and murmuring, sighing and soughing,
Between-times a secretive lullaby-singing –   10
I thought I was hearing ancient sagas,
Age-old charming folktales
Which once as a boy
I heard from the neighbours' children,
When on a summer evening   15
On the stone front doorstep
We crouched down quiet for story-telling,
With small and hearkening hearts
And curious, knowing eyes;
While the big girls   20
Sat at the window opposite
Among fragrant flowerpots,
Rose faces,
Smiling and moonlit.

                                        J.

Questions (1)

By the sea, the wild nocturnal sea,
Stands a stripling-man;
His breast full of woe, his mind full of doubt,
And with gloomy lips he questions the waves:

'O solve me the riddle of life,   5
The torturing ancient riddle
So many heads have brooded upon,
Heads in hieroglyph-covered hats,
In turbans and birettas of black,
Heads bewigged and a thousand more   10
Poor, perspiring human heads –
Tell me, what does Man signify?
Whence does he come? and whither go?
Who dwells up there in the golden stars?'

They murmur, waves, their eternal murmur,   15
The wind it blows, the clouds run free,
The stars shine on, indifferent and cold,
And a fool waits for an answer.

J.

Spring Song (2)

Softly through my mind they throng,
Delicately ringing;
Go then, little springtime song,
To far places winging.

Winging to the distant house   5
Where, with flowers round her,
You will see my lovely rose;
Greet her when you've found her.

J.

Degeneration

Has nature also gone downhill,
And taken on human vices too?
It seems now even flora and fauna
Are lying just as humans do.

The lily, famed for chasteness once,   5
Has started flirting shamelessly;
A butterfly comes fluttering by,
And bang goes her virginity.

The shy retiring violet,
I'm very sorry to assert,   10
Despite the coyness of her scent,
Is just a closet extrovert.

I doubt too if the nightingale
Is quite sincere in what she sings;
All those warbles, trills and sobs   15
Rehearse the same old routine things.

Truth is fading from the world,
And loyalty too has gone to pot.
Dogs still wag their tails and stink,
But faithful, sadly, they are not.   20

D.

Upon this Rock . . .

Upon this rock we now do found
A new church for our day,
The Church of the Third Testament:
Pain shall no more hold sway.

Gone is the old divided self   5
That dogged us for so long,
The foolish torturing of the flesh
At last is proven wrong.

Hark to the thousand voices of
The God in sea and night,   10
And high above us there, behold
His thousand eyes of light.

Our deity is in that light
And in the darkness too;
Our God is everything that is   15
(He's there when I kiss you).

J.

Thanksgiving

Now the god looks down with favour,
Shall I not say I'm delighted,
Having made such lamentations
When my love was unrequited

That a thousand lads wrote verses   5
In the same despairing fashion,
Causing far more trouble than was
Caused to start with by my passion?

Oh you nightingales within me,
Chorus now this revelation,   10
Tell your joy to every hearer
In full-hearted celebration.

                                        J.

Kiss as Kiss can

Myself when young believed the kisses
That a woman gives and takes
Were predestined by decisions
Some primeval power makes.

So I would exchange in earnest   5
Kisses early, kisses late,
Just as if I was performing
Necessary acts of fate.

Now I know that kissing isn't
Part of the eternal plan;   10
Faithless, easy-going, I just
Take as many as I can.

                                        J.

Ash Wednesday

Love's mad Mardi Gras is ended
And our hearts' intoxication, –
Ended, and we sit here sobered,
Yawning in each other's face!

To the lees our cup is emptied   5
That was filled with sensual pleasure,
Foaming, blazing, brimming over;
To the lees it now is drained.

And the violins fall silent,
No more drive us with their urging   10
To the dance, the dance of passion;
Yes, the violins are silent.

See, the lamps too are extinguished
Whose wild light illuminated
All the bright-hued masqueraders;   15
Now the lamps too are extinguished.

And tomorrow is Ash Wednesday.
I will mark you on the forehead
With a cross of ash and say:
'Remember, Woman, thou art dust!'   20

J.

Non-combatant

In galleries you'll often see
The picture of a valiant knight,
Full-armed with sword and shield and lance,
All ready to ride off and fight.

But little cupids ring him round,   5
They tease him, steal his lance and sword,
They bind him fast with flower-chains,
Strive though he may to keep his word.

Just so, delicious hindrances
Have caught me fast in pleasure's lime,   10
Leaving it up to other men
To fight the battle of our time.

                                  J.

from Atta Troll

CANTO III

Summer night's dream, quite fantastic
Is my song, without a purpose,
Purposeless as life or love or
The creation and Creator!

Heeding only its own pleasure,   5
Whether galloping or flying,
Romping in the realm of fable,
My belovèd Pegasus.

Not a virtuous and useful
Carthorse of the bourgeoisie,   10
Nor a warhorse of some party,
Neighing, stamping in its passion.

Golden-shod the hooves are of my
Little white and wingèd charger,
Strings of pearls the reins and bridle,   15
And I let him have his head.

Carry me just where you fancy
Over airy mountain pathways
Where cascades come crashing, warning
Of the dark abyss of nonsense.   20

Carry me through quiet valleys
Where the oak-trees stand so earnest
And the ancient source of sagas
Trickles through the roots' gnarled tangle.

Let me drink my fill, and moisten   25
There my eyes – I feel such yearning

For the wonder-working water
That can give us sight and insight.

And the blindness yields! My vision
Pierces the ravine where Atta   30
Has his cave deep in the mountains,
And I understand his speeches.

How bizarre! For quite familiar
Is this ursine language – did I
Not hear once before these self-same   35
Noises in my cherished homeland?

CANTO V

'Damn them all! These human beings,
Arrogant and proud as any
Aristocracy, look down on
Us, the animal creation,

'Steal our wives and children from us,   5
Chain, ill-treat and even kill us,
And dispose, for filthy lucre,
Of our precious pelt and carcase!

'They believe that they're entitled
To commit these unjust actions   10
On the race of bears especially,
And they call it "human rights".

'Human rights! What rights have humans?
Who on earth was there to grant them?
Certainly it wasn't Nature,   15
Nature isn't so unnatural.

'Human rights! Whoever gave you
These much-vaunted privileges?
Certainly it wasn't Reason,
She's not so unreasonable.   20

'Human beings, are you better
Than the beasts because the victuals
That you eat get boiled or roasted,
While we eat our victuals raw?

'Yet the end-result's no different,   25
So what difference does it make? No,
What you eat does not ennoble,
Noble is as noble does.

'So, what makes you humans better
Than an animal? It's true that   30
You walk upright, hold your head high –
But the thoughts creep low inside it.

'And you needn't think you're better
Just because your pelt is different,
Smooth and shiny – some advantage!   35
That's a thing you share with serpents.

'Human race! two-leggèd serpents,
I know why you wear those trousers,
Stealing wool of other creatures
So you don't go serpent-naked.   40

'Children! don't be taken in by
Misbegotten hairless beings.
O my daughters! trust not monsters
That approach you wearing trousers.'

Well, that's quite enough for now of   45
How the upstart bear attacked us.
What egalitarian nonsense!
What a swindle! What a sauce!

[. . .]

Even so, it's worth informing
Other human beings, being   50

Of a higher beastly status,
Of the sort of thing that's muttered

Down there in the murky lower
Regions of the social order.
In the depths the brutes are brooding,   55
Full of misery, pride, resentment.

Everything ordained by nature
And by customary law, what
Long millennia have hallowed,
Saucy snouts are now denying.   60

Old ones pass it down to young ones,
Grunt and growl the evil doctrines,
Messages that threaten culture
And humanity on earth.

'Children!' – Atta Troll continues,   65
Growling out his doctrine at them,
Tossing, turning on his bed, 'We
Are the party of the future.

'If the bears all thought as I do,
And the other animals,   70
With united forces we would
Fight against the human tyrants.

'Unity! That is the watchword
For our time. They caught us singly
And enslaved us, but united   75
We'll outwit our cruel masters.

'Unity! yes, that's our slogan.
We shall overcome and topple
Humankind's exclusive power,
Found a just realm just for us.   80

'Our first law will state that all God's
Creatures shall be seen as equal,

Irrespective of their creed and
Of their pelt and of their odour.

'Strictly equal! Any ass will   85
Qualify to be Prime Minister,
And the lion will very likely
Carry corn-sacks to the mill.

'There are problems with the dog, though,
Turned into a servile creature   90
By millennia of humans
Treating him just like a dog.

'But when we've restored our freedom,
We will give him back his ancient
Rights and privileges, soon he'll   95
Be again a noble creature.

'In our system, even Jews will
Have full civil rights accorded
And before the law be equal
To all other kinds of mammal.   100

'Only dancing in the market,
That is something Jews may *not* do,
This amendment must be added
In the interests of my art.'

CANTO XXIV

In the vale of Ronceval,
On the selfsame spot where Roland,
Charlemagne's heroic nephew
Long ago breathed out his soul,

There fell also Atta Troll,   5
Fell by ambush vile like Roland,
Whom the evil knightly Judas
Ganelon of Mainz betrayed.

Woe! the noblest part of beardom,
Tender love of ursine partner,   10
Was the snare Uraka's cunning
Used to bring our hero low.

So deceptively she mimicked
Beautiful black Mumma's grunting,
It enticed poor Atta, from the   15
Safety of his bear's lair lured him.

As on wings of yearning flew he
Through the vale, and stood there sniffing
Tenderly before a boulder,
Thought that Mumma there was hiding.   20

But alas! it was Laskaro
Hid there with his musket ready,
Through his happy heart he shot him,
And the blood poured fourth in streams.

Atta's head went waggle, waggle,   25
But at last he tumbled headlong
With a groan and horrid twitchings,
And his final sigh was 'Mumma!'

Thus he fell, our noble hero,
Thus he perished. But immortal   30
He will yet be resurrected
Posthumous in poet's song.

He will rise again in saga
And his fame will strut colossal,
Grandiose in four-foot trochees,   35
Through this little world of ours.

He will have, too, his memorial
From King Ludwig of Bavaria
In the Wittelsbach Valhalla,
In best lapidary phrasing: 40

'Atta Troll! Politbear, moral
And religious, ardent husband;
Through seduction by the zeitgeist
Woodland wild's first freedom-fighter;

'Dancing badly, but conviction   45
Bearing in his shaggy bear's breast,
Proud, though none too seldom stinking,
Talent none, but CHARACTER!'

J.

Tannhäuser, a Legend

I

Good Christians all, lest Satan you
With wicked guile ensnare,
I'll tell you now Tannhäuser's tale
To make your souls beware.

The noble knight Tannhäuser sought 5
Love's pleasures unrestrained,
Betook him to the Venus-Berg
And seven years remained.

'Dame Venus, lovely mistress mine,
Farewell, my dearest life! 10
I will no longer bide with you,
Now part we without strife.'

"Tannhäuser, o my noble knight,
We have not kissed today.
Kiss me, and tell me what you lack 15
That you would ride away.

'Have I not poured you good sweet wine,
Made sweeter by my sharing,
And daily garlanded your brow,
With roses never sparing?' 20

'Dame Venus, lovely lady mine,
From your sweet wine and kisses
The soul within me is grown sick,
I thirst for bitternesses.

'Too much we have jested, too much laughed, 25
Now tears are my desire.

No garlands more, but to a crown
Of thorns I do aspire.'

'Tannhäuser, o my noble knight,
I see you are set on strife,   30
And yet you swore a thousand times
That you were mine for life.

'Come, let us to my chamber in
And play love's secret play;
My lovely body lily-white   35
Shall drive your cares away.'

'Dame Venus, lovely lady mine,
Your charms will ever bless you,
So many men have burned for you,
And many still burn to possess you.   40

'When I think of all the heroes and gods
Who from it had their pleasure,
Your lovely body lily-white,
It quite o'erflows the measure.

'Your lovely body lily-white,   45
To see I cannot bear it
For thinking of the many men
Who still one day will share it.'

'Tannhäuser, oh my noble knight,
I'd sooner far you beat me   50
As you have often done before
Than with hard words ill-treat me.

'I'd sooner far be beaten than
Have insults heaped upon me
By a cold ungrateful Christian who   55
Now takes my last pride from me.

'It comes of loving you too much
That now such words are spoken.

Farewell, I give you leave to go,
The gate myself shall open.'   60

II

In Rome, in the holy City of Rome,
There is ringing of bells and chanting.
Here comes the procession through the streets,
The Pope in its midst advancing.

Pope Urban it is, a pious pope,   5
The threefold crown he is wearing,
And with it he wears a purple robe,
Its train the barons are bearing.

'O Holy Father, Pope Urban, stay,
You shall not go from this spot
Until you have heard my confession first   10
And saved me from hell so hot!'

The people fall back and make a ring,
The priestly chantings cease –
Who is this pilgrim pale and wild?   15
They see him drop to his knees.

'O Holy Father, Pope Urban, stay,
You have power to loose and bind.
Now rescue me from the pains of hell
And the grasp of the evil fiend!   20

'I am the noble Tannhäuser, I sought
Love's pleasures unrestrained,
Betook me to the Venus-Berg
And seven years remained.

'Dame Venus is a lady fair,   25
In grace and charm abounding
Like sunshine and the scent of flowers
Her voice is so soft-sounding.

'As the butterfly hovers at the rim
Of the flower's cup and sips,   30
So too did my soul flutter alway
About her rosy lips.

'The wild black locks luxuriant
Around her face do play;
When she looks at you with those great eyes,   35
It takes your breath away.

'When she looks at you with those great eyes,
You stand as if chained fast.
I only escaped from her mountain place
With desperate effort at last.   40

'Yes, I escaped from her mountain place,
But the beauteous lady's gaze
Pursues me ever and beckons me back
To the old familiar ways.

'A wretched ghost I am by day,   45
I revive at eventide,
For then I dream of my lady fair,
She sits and laughs by my side.

'Her laugh is so healthy, so happy, so free,
Her white teeth flashing bare.   50
I only have to think of her laugh
And I weep the tears of despair.

'My love for her is a mighty force,
A force that nought can stop.
It is like a wild waterfall whose floods   55
Could never be dammed up.

'It rushes down from rock to rock,
It froths and foams and roars,
And though it be broken a thousand times,
Nothing can stay its course.   60

'And if the whole of heaven were mine,
I would lay it at her feet,
I would give her the sun, I would give her the moon
And the constellations complete.

'My love for her is a mighty force,   65
A consuming conflagration.
Is it already the fire of hell,
The flames of eternal damnation?

'O Holy Father, Pope Urban, pray,
You have power to loose and bind.   70
Now rescue me from the pains of hell
And the grasp of the evil fiend!'

The Pope held up his hands in lament,
Lamenting he then did speak:
'Tannhäuser, o unhappy man,   75
This magic nothing can break.

'The Devil called Venus is the worst
Of all, her power such is
That I can rescue you nevermore
From out of her lovely clutches.   80

'Your soul must pay for the lusts of the flesh
That you have enjoyed so well.
You are cast out, you are condemned
To the endless torments of hell.'

III

The noble Tannhäuser travels so fast,
His feet are weary and sore.
It is getting on for midnight when
He arrives at Dame Venus's door.

The lady Venus awoke from sleep,   5
She sprang from her bed apace.

Once more she held the man she loved
In her lovely white embrace.

Then from her nose the blood ran down
And from her eyes the tears.   10
The face of her beloved man
With blood and salt she smears.

The knight he betook him straight to bed,
He said not a word of greeting.
Dame Venus to the kitchen went   15
To cook some soup and feed him.

She gave him soup, she gave him bread,
She washed his wounded feet;
She combed the tangles from his hair,
Her laughter again was sweet.   20

'Tannhäuser, o my noble knight,
You have been long away.
Tell me, what lands have you sojourned in,
What seen this many a day?'

'Dame Venus, lovely mistress mine,   25
I had some business in Rome,
So I saw a good deal of Italy
Before I came hurrying home.

'In Rome we were spread over seven hills,
The Tiber flowed between us.   30
I also saw the Pope in Rome,
He said "Regards to Venus".

'I called at Florence on the way back,
I also took Milan in.
I clambered up Switzerland pretty fast   35
To fit my travel planning.

'And as I came across the Alps
The snow began a-falling,

The lakes had a blue and laughing mien,
The eagles were croaking and calling.   40

'When I stood on the St Gotthard Pass,
I could hear how Germany snored
Down there in the charge of the thirty-six
Mini-monarchs they've restored.

'In Swabia I saw their Poets' School,   45
Such dear little creatures all sitting
Round in their funny little hats
And lyrically shitting.

'The Jewish sabbath in Frankfurt it was,
The tcholent and dumplings were wizard;   50
That really *is* a religion now –
And I love the goose's gizzard.

'In Dresden I saw an ancient hound
Whose better days are *long* gone,
For now his teeth are falling out   55
And barking is all he's strong on.

'In Weimar, the widowed Muses' seat,
I heard much weeping and wailing.
The trouble is that Goethe's dead
And Eckermann's not even ailing.   60

'At Potsdam too the outcry was loud –
"What's up?" I cried on entry.
It was Gans in Berlin who'd been stirring things up
With lectures on our century.

'At Göttingen scholarship's in full bloom,   65
It's fruit it doesn't bear.
It was pitch-black night when I came through,
Not a light anywhere.

'The prison in Celle was full up
With Hanover people – alack!   70

What we Germans don't have is a national jail
And a whip for our common back.

'At Hamburg I asked them why it was
The stench in the streets was so strong.
They blamed the drains, the Christians and Jews　　75
Hadn't done anything wrong.

'Hamburg is really *such* a good town,
It just has the odd shady dweller.
When I called in at the Stock Exchange,
It was rather like being in Celle.　　80

'I also went out to Altona,
That too has salubrious air.
Another time I'll tell you the things
That happened to me there.'

J.

from **Germany**

A Winter's Tale

CANTO I

In the dismal month of November it was,
The gloomy days grew shorter,
The wind was tugging the last leaves down
As I left for the German border.

And as I came nearer German soil,   5
I felt my heart beat quicker
Within my breast, and I even think
A tear began to trickle.

It did strange things to me when I heard
The German language spoken –   10
Like nothing so much as if my heart
Was pleasantly being broken.

A little girl was playing the harp
And singing with genuine feeling
And out of tune, but still the song   15
She sang was most appealing.

She sang of love and sacrifice,
Of pain and a tomorrow
When all shall meet in a better world
Beyond this vale of sorrow;   20

Of how all sufferings will be past,
Each soul will bask transfigured
In joys eternal, not like here
Where pleasures are brief and niggard.

She sang the ancient lullaby   25
Of doing without, of pie-in-

The-sky, that they soothe the people with,
Great oaf, when they hear it crying.

I know the tune, I know the words,
I know every single author;   30
I know they tippled wine on the quiet
While publicly preaching water.

A different song, a better song,
Will get the subject straighter:
Let's make a heaven on earth, my friends,   35
Instead of waiting till later.

Why shouldn't we be happy on earth,
Why should we still go short?
Why should the idle belly consume
What working hands have wrought?   40

There's bread enough grows here on earth
To feed mankind with ease,
And roses and myrtles, beauty and joy,
And (in the season) peas.

Yes, fresh green peas for everyone   45
As soon as the pods have burst.
Heaven we'll leave to the angels, and
The sparrows, who had it first.

And should we find that after death
We've grown some wings, we'll make   50
A point of calling on you up there
For some blessèd tea-and-cake.

A better song, with fiddles and flutes,
To set the people singing!
The miserere is out of date,   55
The death-knell's no longer ringing.

The maiden Europa is betrothed
To that handsome Genius, Freedom.

They lie in each other's arms embraced,
It warms my heart to see them.   60

No priest will bless their vows, but the pair
Have taken and will fulfil them.
Here's to the bride and here's to the groom,
And to all their future children.

That's wedding enough, and I'll sing my song   65
To help the solemnising.
Deep in my heart I feel the stars
Of consecration rising.

They are stars inspired, they wildly glow,
Dissolving in streams of fire –   70
I feel I could break an oak, my strength
Miraculously grows higher.

Since I set foot on German soil
The magic juices are flowing –
The giant has touched his mother again,   75
And he feels his powers growing.

CANTO II

While that musical maiden warbled about
Her heavenly predilection,
The Prussian Customs gave my trunk
The usual prying inspection.

They sniffed and rummaged in shirts and pants   5
To see if I'd something hidden –
Jewels, or Belgian lace, or books
The censor had forbidden.

It's no good poking about, you fools,
Peering and looking worried.   10

The contraband is not in there,
It's safe behind my forehead.

I've something that needles of Malines
And Brussels could not work finer.
You'll find when *my* needles get to work   15
They're sharper and maligner.

And jewels are there, crown jewels, no less,
Of ages that will succeed us,
Temple jewels for an unknown god
When from the old one he's freed us.   20

And books! I'm full of them, like a tree
In spring when the songbirds have nested
And fledglings clamour to take the wing –
Any one would get me arrested.

You'd not find books on Satan's shelves   25
Of upheaval more precursive,
That Hoffmann von Fallersleben chap
Hasn't been more subversive.

Another passenger standing near
Remarked that what I was seeing   30
Was the famous Prussian Zollverein,
The Great Chain of Well-being.

'The Customs Union,' he opined,
'Will be our people's foundation,
And make the divided fatherland   35
Into a single nation.

'This outward unity is our first
Since the empire of you-know-when, sir.
The higher unity of ideas
Is the task we leave to the censor.   40

'Yes, inner unity is his job,
We must all think as he allows us.

Germany one, without and within —
That's the ideal to rouse us.'

CANTO XI

This is the forest of Teutoburg,
You probably know it from Tacitus.
This is where Varus got himself stuck,
The classic boggy morass it was.

The Cheruscan prince defeated him here,   5
Arminius, alias Hermann;
The German principle won the day,
The muck was also German.

Just think, if Arminius's blond horde
Had lost to the foreign foeman,   10
Would German liberty be what it is?
We should have all been Roman.

Rome's language and Rome's ways would reign,
There'd be vestal virgins in Munich,
Those dear little Swabians would look so sweet   15
In Roman toga or tunic.

We'd have Hengstenberg as a haruspex,
Over ox's offal pondering,
And Neander as augur on the watch
For flocks of wild birds wandering.   20

Birch-Pfeiffer'd be swigging turpentine,
Like Rome's ladies aristocratic.
(It's said that a side effect was to make
Their urine aromatic.)

Raumer would not be a German clod,   25
He'd be a Roman Clodius;

Freiligrath's poems would have no rhymes,
Though they'd be no more melodious.

There'd be a Latin name for Father
Jahn, that vulgar bully.   30
Me Hercule! Massmann would hold forth
In polished Latin like Tully.

Lovers of truth would have to fight
With jackals, lions and hyenas,
And not – as now – with dogs in trivial   35
Journalistic arenas.

We'd have a single Nero now
Instead of princes in dozens.
We'd slit a vein to escape his spite
Like our noble Roman cousins.   40

Schelling would nobly take his life
In line with Seneca's dictum.
We'd look at Cornelius' pictures and say:
'*Cacatum non est pictum.*'

Thank God! The Romans were beaten then,   45
Soundly enough to deter them.
Varus with all his legions was lost,
And Germany stayed German.

Germans we stayed, and Germans we are,
And German's the language we gas in –   50
A German says 'ass', not 'asinus'
(He has ways to be an ass in).

Raumer remained a German clod,
They even gave him a medal.
Freiligrath isn't a Horace, of course;   55
He just has his rhymes to peddle.

Massmann, praise be, knows no Latin at all,
Birch-Pfeiffer's penchant is dramatic,

She needn't tipple turpentine
To be aristo-aromatic.   60

O Hermann, for all this we've you to thank!
So at Detmold, as is fitting,
They're building you a monument –
I've even put my bit in.

CANTO XII

It is night. Our chaise bumps on through the woods.
Suddenly there's a cracking –
A wheel's come off. We stop. All's still.
This is a bit nerve-racking.

Off the postilion goes – how far   5
Will the nearest village or town be?
It's midnight. I am alone in the wood.
A howling starts up all around me.

That's the wolves, their howling is wild,
They sound as if they're ravenous.   10
I see their fiery eyes aglow
All round in the darkness cavernous.

It seems the news of my approach
Has travelled on before us.
It's for me they've illuminated the wood,   15
And now they're singing a chorus.

It's a serenade. Ah! now I see,
They're treating me to the red carpet.
I strike a pose and make a speech,
With emotional gestures to mark it: ·   20

'Dear fellow wolves! To be in your midst
Today makes me truly happy –
And to have so many noble minds
Howling lovingly at me.

'The feelings that this moment inspires 25
Are the kind that never perish.
Yes! This is one of the hours, I know,
That my heart will always cherish.

'I thank you for the trust which you
Reposed in me. It was knowing 30
In testing times of your unfail-
Ing support that kept me going.

'My friends! You never doubted me,
You never let rascals deceive you
Who spread the tale that I was well in 35
With the dogs and planned to leave you,

'That I was a traitor, after high rank
Among the Sheepish nation –
I didn't consider such rumours deserved
The honour of refutation. 40

'If ever I put sheep's clothing on,
It was purely a practical measure,
It kept me warm, but I never felt
That Sheepdom afforded much pleasure.

'I'm not a sheep, I'm not a dog, 45
Not after high rank, not selfish –
I've always remained a wolf, my heart
And these teeth of mine are wolfish.

'A wolf – I shall always howl with you
From no more than a little distance. 50
So count on me and help yourselves,
The Lord will add his asssistance.'

That was the speech I made – a speech
Is always improvisable.
Kolb's *Allgemeine* printed it: 55
It was quite unrecognisable.

CANTO XXVI

The Goddess's cheeks were red and flushed –
The rum, I think, was doing it –
And thus she spoke, in saddened tones,
As if she was already ruing it:

'I grow old, I was born when first they built   5
This city, and "Hamburg" called it.
My mother was a shellfish queen
Where the Elbe flows into the Baltic.

'My father was great Charlemagne,
The lord of a mighty kingdom.   10
He had even more power than Frederick the Great
Of Prussia, and much more wisdom.

'The throne he sat on the day he was crowned
Is still in Aachen; the other,
The one he sometimes sat on at night,   15
Was left to my dear late mother.

'My mother left it in turn to me:
As antiques go, there are finer,
But I wouldn't swap it for Rothschild's bank
Or for all the tea in China.   20

'It's over there in the corner, look,
Just an old chair; the leather
Is worn and torn on the arms, the seat
Is moth-eaten altogether.

'But if you go across and lift   25
The cushion from the settle,
You'll see a circular opening,
And beneath it a pot made of metal.

'That is a magic pot, wherein
The occult forces are brewing;   30

If you put your head down the hole, it will be
The future you are viewing –

'The future of Germany you will see
Down there like a shifting phantasma,
But do not shudder if the filth   35
Sends up a foul miasma!'

Thus she spake, and laughed a strange laugh;
But I was not to be daunted.
Curious, I hastened to peer through the hole,
To see what terrors would haunt it.   40

What I saw, I will not betray,
For I promised never to tell it.
But seeing was only half the tale –
Ye gods! if you could smell it! . . .

It still revolts me when I recall   45
The smells I smelt to begin with –
The stink of untanned hides, and of old
Bad cabbage it was mixed in with.

But the scents that followed this prelude, God!
Were anything but respites;   50
It smelt as if they were sweeping the dung
From six-and-thirty cesspits.

I know that curing a great disease
Is harder than one supposes –
As Saint-Just once said, you don't get far   55
With musk and oil of roses.

But the way the German future smelt
Was ghastly, hideous – stronger
Than ever my nose had bargained for –
Soon I could stand it no longer . . .   60

I lost my senses, and when once more
I opened my eyes, the Goddess

Was there beside me, my head reposed
Upon her buxom bodice.

Her eyes were flashing, her lips aglow,   65
Her breath came fast and frantic;
She sang a wild ecstatic song
As she clasped me in embrace bacchantic:

'Stay with me in Hamburg, I love you, let's
Attend to the eating and drinking of   70
Oysters and wine in the present, the dark
German future doesn't bear thinking of.

'Put back the lid! It would dampen our joys
If that smell crept out from below it.
I love you as hotly as woman e'er loved   75
A handsome German poet.

'The moment I kiss you, I'm carried away
By poetic inspiration,
I feel my soul is in the grip
Of a wondrous intoxication.   80

'I seem to hear out there in the street
The nightwatchmen singing for us –
Sweet partner in pleasure, they're marriage songs,
An epithalamial chorus!

'And now I see mounted servants appear,   85
With torches suggestively flickering,
They dance the torch-dance to honour us,
Jumping and prancing and wiggling.

'The City Elders and Senate are come,
That reverend institution;   90
The Burgomaster clears his throat
To pronounce an allocution.

'The corps of diplomats appears,
They're resplendent for the formalities

And (with some reservations) wish us well 95
In the name of their principalities.

'The rabbis and pastors are here in force
To represent things religious –
Oh dear! here's Censor Hoffmann too,
And he's brought his official scissors! 100

'The scissors are clicking in his hand –
He's wild, he's foaming, he's hissing –
He rushes up to you – there's a snip –
Alack! now your best piece is missing.'

J.

The Political Poets

German singer! Sing the praise
Of German freedom! Let your song
Lift our souls to high endeavour,
And to deeds will live for ever,
Rather like the Marseillaise.   5

Not like love-lorn Werther's cooing
When for Lotte once he longed,
Tell the nation what it's time for,
What else do you have your rhyme for?
Speak now daggers, swords! Be doing!   10

Not the flute, whose gentle trilling
To idyllic scenes belongs –
Take the nation's drum and thump it,
Be the cannon, be the trumpet,
Blowing, blasting, thund'ring, killing!   15

Blast them daily – oh, terrific! –
Till the last oppressor's gone.
That's the poet's true direction.
But with proper circumspection
Mind it isn't too specific.   20

J.

No Need to Worry

We're just like Brutus, fast asleep.
But Brutus woke, and buried deep
In Caesar's breast the cold bright steel:
Rome carved its tyrants as a meal.

We're no Romans, we like a smoke.   5
Tastes do differ from folk to folk;
Every people is great at something:
Swabians cook you a nifty dumpling.

We're Germans, people you can trust,
We lie here sleeping the sleep of the just.   10
We wake with a thirst, that's the usual thing,
But not for the blood of a prince or a king.

Sturdy and true like the oak are we,
Or like the linden, our favourite tree.
In the land where the oak and linden sprout,   15
There aren't many Brutuses about.

The Roman Brutus had things easier.
A Brutus here would find no Caesar,
No single ruler at our head.
We have a nice line in gingerbread.   20

Full six-and-thirty our rulers are
(That's none too many!) and a star
Protects each heart – they needn't fear
The fateful Ides of March each year.

We call them 'fathers', it's 'fatherland',   25
Which makes it easy to understand
Why it all belongs to them, and we
Have sausage and sauerkraut for tea.

When 'father' passes with princely tread,
We raise our hat and bow our head.   30
Germany's far too home-sweet-home
To do the deeds they did in Rome.

J.

Promise

German liberty! No longer
Must you go barefoot through bogs,
You're to get some socks – and clogs!
(Nice to be in something stronger.)

On your head they're now bestowing   5
Jolly hats all warm and woolly,
So you'll be protected fully
When the winter wind starts blowing.

Fodder too will soon be ample.
What a future lies before you!   10
Just beware the French, make sure you
Aren't seduced by their example.

Audacity? Now don't you dare!
Authority you still must bow to,
All the nobs you must kow-tow to.   15
(Quick! there's his Worship the Lord Mayor!)

J.

King Ludwig to King Frederick William IV

Brother of the Prussian line,
Don't be cross now Lola's mine:
You mustn't mind if I parade it,
Just because you never made it.

J.

The Silesian Weavers

Not a tear in their eye but faces of doom,
And their teeth are bared as they tread the loom:
'Germany, this is your shroud we weave,
The pattern – three curses with no reprieve.
We are weaving, weaving.   5

'A curse on the idol we prayed to of old
In the torments of hunger, in winter's cold.
We gritted our teeth and hoped in vain,
He fooled us and mocked us and fooled us again.
We are weaving, weaving.   10

'A curse on the king of the rich and the great
Who was blind to the misery at his gate,
Who squeezed us for every penny we'd got
Till we rose, and like dogs he had us shot.
We are weaving, weaving.   15

'A curse on the homeland that's no such place
For us whose lives are its shame and disgrace,
Where the bloom is broken and falls by the way,
Where all is corruption, mould and decay.
We are weaving, weaving.   20

'The creaking loom and the shuttle's flight,
We weave unceasing day and night.
Old Germany, it is your shroud we weave,
The pattern – three curses with no reprieve.
We are weaving, weaving.'   25

J.

Life's Voyage

Oh, the laughing and singing! The play of the light
As we rocked on the waves when the world was right,
Oh that nice little boat where I sat reclined
With friends I loved and an easy mind!

The boat got smashed into fragments of wood,   5
As swimmers my friends were none too good,
They sank back home with never a trace,
The storm cast me up in this foreign place.

I've boarded another boat here on the Seine
With a crew of new friends; and once again   10
I'm out on the water, I'm pitched and tossed.
How heavy my heart for the homeland I lost.

And once again there is laughter and song –
But the wind is rising, the planks aren't strong –
The clouds have hidden the last pale star.   15
My heart how heavy! My homeland how far!

J.

Night Thoughts

I think of Germany in the night
And all my sleep is put to flight.
I cannot get my eyes to close,
The stream of burning teardrops flows.

The years they come, the years they pass.   5
When did I see my mother last?
I saw her last twelve years ago,
I feel my love and longing grow.

My love for her grows ceaselessly,
She's cast some kind of spell on me.   10
I think about her night and day,
God keep the old lady safe, I pray.

So dearly does she love me still,
Her anxious feelings for me fill
Her letters – see the trembling hand?   15
A mother's heart, you understand.

My mother's always in my mind.
Twelve long long years now lie behind,
Twelve long long years with all their harms
Since last I held her in my arms.   20

Germany's healthy as can be,
That land will last eternally!
If I went back there any time,
I'd find those woods of oak and lime.

But could I thirst so to return   25
Without the one for whom I yearn?
The fatherland is there for ay,
My mother though may fail and die.

Of oh so many since I left,
So many friends I'm now bereft,   30
The friends I loved – beyond recall.
My soul bleeds when I count them all.

And count I must, the numbers swell,
My inner torment grows as well,
I think I feel their corpses sprawl   35
On me! Thank God! They yield, they fall!

Thank God! now through my window dance
The morning sunbeams here in France;
In comes my wife, as fresh as day,
And smiles the German cares away.   40

J.

The New Jewish Hospital In Hamburg

A hospital for Jews, for poor sick Jews,
For creatures who are triply suffering,
Burdened with the three infirmities
Of poverty and pain and Jewishness.

But of these three the third one is the worst,   5
The family curse that lasts a thousand years,
The plague brought from the valley of the Nile,
The unhygienic old Egyptian faith.

Nothing exists to heal this deadly ill,
Not steam-baths, water-cures, or surgery,   10
Nor all the multifarious medicines
This clinic offers to its sickly inmates.

Will time, Great Healer, ever purge away
The tainted curse for ever handed on
From father down to son? Will grandchild yet   15
Be brought to health, surviving whole and well?

This we cannot know! But in the meantime
Let us honour one who wisely sought
To mitigate where mitigate one can,
Pouring timely balm on open wounds.   20

This worthy man! He built a hospice here
For those afflictions which are tractable
By the physician's arts (or those of death!)
And saw to beds, to victuals and to care.

A man of deeds, he did what he could do,   25
And in the evening of his life he gave
The hard-earned means to pay for such good works,
And by these alms found respite from his toils.

His gifts were freely given with open hand,
But from his eyes rolled richer gifts than these: 30
The priceless tears that sometimes this man wept
For his and all his brothers' fell disease.

D.

In October 1849

The storm-wind's dropped, and things at home
Again are quiet as can be.
Germany's still a child at heart;
Once more it can enjoy its Christmas tree.

We're playing Happy Families now;   5
It's not allowed to ask for more.
The bird of peace is back again;
It nests beneath the eaves as once before.

The rivers and the woods lie bathed
In moonlight through the still night hours.   10
Hark! What was that? Was it a gun?
Perhaps they've shot another friend of ours.

Perhaps the hothead couldn't wait
To fight again another day.
(Not everyone has so much sense   15
As Horace, who so boldly ran away.)

Or was it just fireworks going off,
Part of the 'Goethe's birthday' rave,
With singers no one's seen for years
Making a come-back (surely from the grave?)   20

Liszt too is back again, alive,
Not lying in his blood, not Franz,
On some Hungarian battlefield
Cut down by Prussian or Croatian hands.

Hungary meanwhile bleeds to death –   25
Is this the last of freedom's wars? –
But knightly Franz came off unharmed,
His sabre still lies in his chest of drawers.

So Franz lives on, as also will
The wondrous tales he's got in store   30

To tell grandchildren at his knee:
'Here I lay and thus my point I bore'.

I only have to hear the word
'Hungary', and my German breast
Swells with emotion's tide, I hear   35
Heroic trumpets calling from the east.

The saga of the heroes stirs
And rings within my mind again,
The old wild song of iron men,
That tells of how the Nibelungs were slain.   40

It is the same heroic doom,
The same old tale is told today,
The names are altered, but it's still
The self-same heroes perish in the fray.

And destiny is still the same: 45
Though proudly freedom's banner flies,
The crude and brutal forces win,
It is the hero who, as ever, dies.

This time the Austrian Ox has made
An ally even of the Bear.   50
Take comfort, Magyar, though you fall –
We have a far worse badge of shame to wear.

For those at least were honest beasts
Who overcame you in fair fight,
Where over us the wolves and swine   55
And common curs now wield unchallenged might.

The creatures howl, they yelp, they grunt,
The victors' stench I cannot bear.
Quiet, poet, lest it get to you.
You're sick enough. Say nothing, and beware.   60

J.

King David

Despots *in articulo*
Smile as they die, for well they know
Power only changes hands.
Human bondage never ends.

Hapless folk! like ox and nag   5
Ceaselessly the cart they drag;
If they rise against the yoke, an
Instant and their neck is broken.

David on his dying day
Speaks to Solomon: By the way,   10
Of my generals, Joab's one
That you need to watch, my son.

Brave as any in the land,
But a man I couldn't stand.
Somehow, though, I couldn't manage   15
To do Joab any damage.

You, my son, are pious, wise,
Mighty, favoured in God's eyes,
And I'm sure you'll get that hated
General Joab liquidated.   20

J.

Doom and Gloom

Lady Luck is rather fickle,
If she comes, she doesn't stay;
She'll give you just a little tickle,
Kiss you, and then slip away.

With Mrs Doom you needn't worry,   5
With her it's just the opposite;
She'll say she's not in any hurry,
And settle by your bed, and knit.

D.

Final Causes

As medieval yobbishness
Became the culture of today,
The piano was of course the thing
Above all else that paved the way.

But railways too have played their role   5
In civilizing family life;
They let you gain the longer view
With distance on domestic strife.

It's something that I much regret
That spinal illness will prevent   10
My growing old in such a world
Of progress and self-betterment.

D.

Double Vision

A mist of mountains, moors and woods
Whirls round inside my brain,
And only slowly does the scene
Assume a grittier grain.

The town I see emerging looks   5
Like Godesberg to me;
I'm sitting there, outside the inn,
Beneath the linden tree.

My throat is dry, as if I'd drunk
The sunset in the sky.   10
Waiter! Waiter! Bring some hock!
The best that money can buy!

The noble juice flows into me
And sets my soul afloat;
Along the way, it also soothes   15
The sunburn in my throat.

A second bottle, waiter, please!
The first went down too fast!
With such a vintage one should pay
Due deference to the past.   20

From here I can see the Drachenfels,
In the sun's last lingering rays;
Its ruins are mirrored in the Rhine
In a blue romantic haze.

With this, the distant vintners' song,   25
And the chirping of birds in the trees,
I find I'm knocking back the wine
With absent-minded ease.

Sometimes I savour the bouquet
As fully as I ought,   30
Sometimes I swig a bucketful
Without a second thought.

And then the strangest thing occurs:
Myself is suddenly gone,
Another me is slurping wine,   35
And I'm just looking on.

This double of mine looks far from well,
He's pale and thin and sick;
He eyes me with a deep disdain
That soon gets on my wick.   40

The fellow claims that he is me,
And goes on to discuss
The fever that we're suffering from,
Us both, the one of us.

We aren't in Godesberg at all,   45
But propped up in a bed
In some Parisian hospital.
A bare-faced lie! I said.

I'll have you know my blooming health
Is like a blooming rose;   50
I'm strong enough to knock you flat;
Stop getting up my nose!

He shrugged and sighed: 'You stupid fool!'
That really made me mad.
I lashed out at this other me   55
With all the strength I had.

But, strangely, every hit I made,
And every punch I threw,
Just landed back on me myself,
And thumped me black and blue.   60

My poor old throat got doubly parched
With all this knockabout;
And when I try to call for wine,
The words just won't come out.

My mind's confused, the world goes black,　　65
I lie here comatose;
A doctor's voice prescribes my drugs,
And specifies the dose.

D.

Gently Does It

And once you're dead, you're in your grave
A long long time – a grim reflection.
I think there might be quite a wait
Before I get my resurrection.

Once more, before the light goes out,   5
Before my heart has ceased to beat,
Once more before I die, I'd like
To worship at a damsel's feet.

A blonde, I have to stipulate,
With eyes as gentle as the moon –   10
The wild brunettes, those burning suns,
I got away from none too soon.

The young are full of sap, they know
What's what, they want their passion's fill,
They rage and swear and make a scene   15
And put each other through the mill.

Un-young and really not quite fit
To undertake a grand reprise,
Once more I'd like to fall in love
And feel the bliss – but quietly, please.   20

J.

Snail's Pace

How very slowly it creeps on
Does time, the hideous gastropod!
But I, entirely motionless,
I stay here on the selfsame spot.

Into this cell there falls no ray   5
Of sun or hope to break the gloom.
Now only for the grave, I know,
Shall I exchange this dreadful room.

Maybe I died here long ago,
Maybe it's just a pack of ghosts,   10
These coloured fantasies to which
At night my arid brain is host.

Spectres indeed they well may be
Of the old pagan pantheon –
Where better should they sport than in   15
A poet's skull who's dead and gone?

Their orgies sweet that thrill the spine,
Mad ghostly revels of the night,
Sometimes the poet-corpse's hand
Tries to write down by morning light.   20

J.

Questions (2)

Cut the pious parables,
The holy hypothetical,
Let's have some answers, could we?
Or would that be too heretical?

Why does the just man always end up   5
Dragging by with cross on shoulder,
While the evil victor sits there
High on horse and ever bolder?

Who's to blame? Not the Almighty,
Surely – couldn't he prevent it?   10
Must we face the grimmer fact that
It was God himself who meant it?

They're the things we go on asking
Till we can't ask any farther
For the earth that stops our mouths – but   15
Is that what you call an answer?

J.

Morphine

Great is the likeness of these beautiful
Two youthful figures even though the one
Is paler far, severer in appearance,
I would say almost more aristocratic
Than is the other, who enfolded me   5
In his embrace, so intimate, so blissful
His smile! Then it would chance the wreath of poppies
That crowned his head would also touch my forehead
And, strangely scented, drive away the anguish
Within my soul – Yet such alleviation   10
Is brief; and I will not recover fully
Until the final sinking of the torch that
His brother holds, whose face is pale and earnest.
To sleep is good, and death is better, but
Far better still never to have been born.   15

J.

It Goes Out

The curtain falls, the show is done,
The people file out one by one.
I wonder, did they like the play?
I heard *some* clapping, anyway.
My audience of so many nights   5
Was showing me its gratitude.
Now all is still, the fun and lights
Have vanished with the multitude.

But listen! Back there in the wings,
A nasty sound of something giving,   10
As if some ancient fiddle-string
Had played its last note to the living.
There's rustling in the stalls, as though
The rats are flitting to and fro.
A rancid smell hangs in the air.   15
A single house-light in despair
Hisses and groans and finally
Goes out. That last poor light was me.

J.

Commemoration

There'll be no mass, no candles lighted,
Kaddish will not be recited,
Everyone will save their breath
On the days that mark my death.

Maybe, though, if spring is stirring   5
And my day is just recurring,
My Mathilde will take a walk to
Montmartre with a friend to talk to.

She'll have artificial flowers
For the gravestone where I lie,   10
And she'll heave a sigh, 'Pauvre homme!'
Wistful moisture in her eye.

It's a long way up, and when she
Gets here, I've alas! poor sweet,
Nothing like a chair to offer,   15
And she's dropping on her feet.

Sweet fat child, you mustn't think of
Walking home in that tired state.
Look, there are some hansoms standing
Down there just outside the gate.   20

J.

Notes

Belshazzar See the biblical account in Daniel 5.

from ATTA TROLL
    Canto XXIV: ll.1–8 In the vale ... betrayed: the mock epic culminates in this incongruous link with the medieval French *Chanson de Roland*. **l.11 Uraka** and **l.21 Laskaro:** a witch and a huntsman – invented figures standing for the forces of reaction that pursued subversives. **ll.38–48 King Ludwig of Bavaria ... talent none but Character!:** Ludwig of Bavaria did write commemorative verse, in a bizarre style which the German here mockingly mimics. The last line reverses the judgement some of Heine's contemporaries passed on him (see introduction, p. xxii).

Tannhäuser: A Legend The who's who of the later stanzas in Section III is less important to the modern reader than the obvious shifts of intention and tone.
    Section III: ll.59–60 The trouble is that Goethe's dead/ And Eckermann's not even ailing: the poet Goethe died in 1832; his amanuensis Eckermann published the first two parts of his *Conversations with Goethe in the Last Years of his Life* in 1837.

from GERMANY
    Canto I: l.75 the giant: one of Hercules' labours was to kill the giant Antaeus, whose strength was renewed if he touched his mother Earth.
    Canto II: l.27 Hoffmann von Fallersleben: contemporary political poet. **l.31 Prussian Zollverein:** the Customs Union was a Prussian initiative, taken in 1828 to create some economic unity between German states. **l.38 the empire of you-know-when:** the so-called Holy Roman Empire of the German Nation, the only form of (loose and largely ineffective) German unity before Bismarck's unification in 1871, was dissolved by Napoleon in 1806. **l.40 the censor:** strict censorship laws were among the repressive measures taken by the German princes in the Karlsbad Decrees of 1819.
    Canto XI: l.6 Arminius, alias Hermann: an ancient vanquisher of a Roman army. **l.17 Hengstenberg:** protestant Professor of Theology in Berlin. **l.19 Neander:** Professor of Evangelical Church History in Berlin.

l.21 Birch-Pfeiffer: actress and author of light plays. **l.25 Raumer:** jurist and historian, of harmless revolutionary pretensions. **l.27 Freiligrath:** one of the would-be political poets. **ll.29–30 Father Jahn:** Friedrich Ludwig Jahn, founder of the German gymnastics movement, which aimed at regeneration, physical and moral, of the German people during the French occupation and was thus a kind of covert resistance organisation. **l.31 Massmann:** another patriotic gymnast and specialist in Germanic studies. **l.41 Schelling:** philosopher, deeply suspect in Heine's eyes as the first to move from abstruse metaphysics to a justification of the existing social order; **Cornelius:** painter, of the Nazarene school which inclined to religious allegory. **l.44 *Cacatum non est pictum:*** 'Shitting isn't painting'.

Canto XII: l.55 Kolb's *Allgemeine*: Kolb was editor-in-chief of the *Ausburger Allgemeine Zeitung* in which Heine published a good deal of his journalism, especially the articles which later made up the volumes *Conditions in France* of 1832 (reports on the aftermath of the July Revolution) and *Lutezia* of 1854.

Canto XXVI: Heine's journey through Germany ends in Hamburg, where he visits his mother and his publisher, meets his dear old censor again, and has a nocturnal encounter with Hammonia, the city's patron goddess. **l.55 Saint-Just:** French revolutionary politician and close associate of Robespierre.

***The Political Poets* l.6 Werther:** the archetypal unhappy lover, from Goethe's tragic novel *The Sufferings of Young Werther* (1774). **l.10 Speak now daggers, swords!:** an echo of *Hamlet* III.ii.427: 'I will speak daggers to her, but not use them', reinforcing the point that the bombast is taking the place of action. Heine's irony is a not wholly reliable weapon – critics have been known to take the poem as a serious exhortation.

***No Need to Worry* ll.1–4 We're just like Brutus ... as a meal:** another echo of Shakespeare. In Act 2 of *Julius Caesar* a letter is thrown through Brutus' window: 'Brutus, thou sleep'st: awake and see thyself [. . .] Speak, strike, redress' (II.i.45–6). The Roman contrast structures Heine's poem.

King Ludwig to King Frederick William IV Satirists like to insinuate their victim is impotent. The imagined tension between the two rulers is over the King of Bavaria's mistress, the adventuress Lola Montez.

The Silesian Weavers The starving Silesian weavers' riots in 1844 were put down by Prussian military force.

The New Jewish Hospital in Hamburg This hospital was founded by Heine's uncle Salomon, an opulent banker, in memory of his late wife Betty, née Goldschmidt. It stood in what is now Simon-van-Utrecht-Strasse in Sankt Pauli, and was opened in 1843.

In October 1849 l.16 **Horace:** The Roman poet Horace fled at the Battle of Philippi (see *Odes* II, vii, stanza 3). **l.18 'Goethe's birthday' rave:** 1849 was the hundredth anniversary of Goethe's birth. **l.21ff. Liszt:** it is not clear why Heine singles out the Hungarian composer for lacking solidarity with his compatriots' revolution. **l.32 'Here I lay and thus my point I bore':** the words put into Liszt's mouth are part of Falstaff's prevarication after he runs away from his friends' mock-ambush at Gad's Hill in *Henry IV*, Part 1, II, iv.

King David Heine's source is the Bible, 1 Kings 2, verses 5ff, and 28ff.

Questions (2) ll.9–12: In this stanza Heine paradoxically clinches his point with a half-rhyme, which suggests the failure of answers to match human questions.

Morphine The unrhymed pentameters are a rare departure from Heine's usual brisk metres and give this poem a dreamy gravity. **l.12 the final sinking of the torch:** the youth turning down a torch to extinguish the flame is an allegorical figure used in antiquity to represent death.

Commemoration l.2 **Kaddish:** the orthodox Jewish memorial prayer. **l.7 My Mathilde:** for all Heine's claimed erotic adventures during his years in Paris, he soon settled down permanently with Eugénie Crescence Mirat, whom he called Mathilde.

Everyman's Poetry

Titles available in this series

William Blake
ed. Peter Butter
0 460 87800 X

The Brontës
ed. Pamela Norris
0 460 87864 6

Rupert Brooke & Wilfred Owen
ed. George Walter
0 460 87801 8

Robert Burns
ed. Donald Low
0 460 87814 X

Lord Byron
ed. Jane Stabler
0 460 87810 7

John Clare
ed. R. K. R. Thornton
0 460 87823 9

Samuel Taylor Coleridge
ed. John Beer
0 460 87826 3

Four Metaphysical Poets
ed. Douglas Brooks-Davies
0 460 87857 3

Oliver Goldsmith
ed. Robert L. Mack
0 460 87827 1

Thomas Gray
ed. Robert Mack
0 460 87805 0

Ivor Gurney
ed. George Walter
0 460 87797 6

Heinrich Heine
ed. T. J. Reed & David Cram
0 460 87865 4

George Herbert
ed. D. J. Enright
0 460 87795 X

Robert Herrick
ed. Douglas Brooks-Davies
0 460 87799 2

John Keats
ed. Nicholas Roe
0 460 87808 5

Henry Wadsworth Longfellow
ed. Anthony Thwaite
0 460 87821 2

Andrew Marvell
ed. Gordon Campbell
0 460 87812 3

John Milton
ed. Gordon Campbell
0 460 87813 1

Edgar Allan Poe
ed. Richard Gray
0 460 87804 2

Poetry Please!
Foreword by Charles Causley
0 460 87824 7

Alexander Pope
ed. Douglas Brooks-Davies
0 460 87798 4

Alexander Pushkin
ed. A. D. P. Briggs
0 460 87862 X

Lord Rochester
ed. Paddy Lyons
0 460 87819 0

Christina Rossetti
ed. Jan Marsh
0 460 87820 4

William Shakespeare
ed. Martin Dodsworth
0 460 87815 8

John Skelton
ed. Greg Walker
0 460 87796 8

Alfred, Lord Tennyson
ed. Michael Baron
0 460 87802 6

R. S. Thomas
ed. Anthony Thwaite
0 460 87811 5

Walt Whitman
ed. Ellman Crasnow
0 460 87825 5

Oscar Wilde
ed. Robert Mighall
0 460 87803 4